THE REALITY
OF MAN

EXCERPTS FROM WRITINGS OF

BAHÁ'U'LLÁH

and

'ABDU'L-BAHÁ

W9-AGH-411

APPROVED BY THE BAHÁ'Í REVIEWING COMMITTEE

BAHÁ'Í PUBLISHING COMMITTEE
P. O. BOX 348, GRAND CENTRAL ANNEX
NEW YORK
1939

First Edition, April 1931
Second Edition, April 1935
Third Edition, August 1939

CONTENTS

INTRODUCTION vii

WORDS OF WISDOM 3

THE POWER OF THOUGHT 9

UNDERSTANDING 10

THE THREE DEGREES OF REALITY 12

SOUL, MIND AND SPIRIT 15

NATURE 18

NATURAL AND SPIRITUAL MAN 24

EVOLUTION OF THE SOUL 26

IMMORTALITY 28

THE DIVINE SPIRIT 35

NATURE AND THE WORD 39

THE MEDIATOR 45

THE MYSTERY OF SACRIFICE 47

SPIRITUAL TRUTH IS REVEALED 53

THE WORLD OF GOD 57

INTRODUCTION

IN every great crisis of human affairs, the fundamental point at issue turns upon differences in our conception of the nature of man. However the issue is clothed in political, economic or social terms—however unconscious the mass of people may seem to be that it is man himself at stake—no true solution is arrived at until the spiritual problem has been cleared.

The great issues before the world today, such as the struggle between nationalism and internationalism, the problem of religious unity and the bitter conflict between capitalist and communist economic theories, all serve to reveal profound chasms in our spiritual philosophy. The question: what is man? confronts us at every turn, and the age is one of vital crisis for the very reason that this question cannot be postponed nor evaded any more.

The message of Bahá'u'lláh, dealing as it does with the nature of man from a universal point of view, assumes ever greater significance as men penetrate the superficial aspects of the modern controversy and realize that the supreme problem is whether man has reached the end of his evolution or has a future transcending his past; whether social relationships are based upon compulsory obedience to arbitrary authority or upon mutual loyalties and voluntary cooperation.

Although the present compilation offers but a few coins from the abundant wealth of that message, these coins are purest gold. To the bankruptcy of modern thought they bring a power of assurance, a measure of reality, that outweighs the poverty of a world at the end of its own resources.

HORACE HOLLEY

New York City
January 11, 1930

BAHÁ'U'LLÁH

THE REALITY OF MAN

WORDS OF WISDOM

I

THE source of all good is trust in God, submission unto His command, and contentment in His holy will and pleasure.

The essence of wisdom is the fear of God, the dread of His scourge and the apprehension of His justice and decree.

The essence of religion is to testify unto that which the Lord hath revealed, and follow that which He hath ordained in His mighty Book.

The source of all glory is acceptance of whatsoever the Lord hath bestowed, and contentment with that which God hath ordained.

The essence of love is for man to turn his heart to the Beloved One, and sever himself from all else but God, and desire naught save that which is the desire of his Lord.

True remembrance is to make mention of the Lord, the All-Praised, and forget all else beside Him.

True reliance is for the servant to pursue his profession and calling in this world, to hold fast unto the Lord, to seek naught but His grace, inasmuch as in His hands is the destiny of all His servants.

The essence of detachment is for man to turn his face toward the courts of the Lord, to enter His presence, behold His countenance, and stand as witness before Him.

The essence of understanding is to testify to one's poverty, and submit to the will of the Lord, the Sovereign, the Gracious, the All-Powerful.

The source of courage and power is the promotion of the Word of God, and steadfastness in His Love.

The essence of charity is for the servant to recount the blessings of his Lord, and to render thanks unto Him at all times, and under all conditions.

The essence of wealth is love for Me. Whoso loveth Me is the possessor of all things, and he that loveth Me not is, indeed, of the poor and needy. This is that which the Finger of Glory and Splendor hath revealed. . . .

The essence of faith is fewness of words and abundance of deeds; he whose words exceed his deeds, know verily his death is better than his life. . . .

The source of all evil is for man to turn away from his Lord and set his heart on things ungodly.

The most burning fire is to question the signs of God, to dispute idly that which He hath revealed, to deny Him and carry one's self proudly before Him.

The source of all learning is the knowledge of God, exalted be His Glory, and this cannot be attained save through the knowledge of His Divine Manifestation. The essence of abasement is to pass from under the shadow of the Merciful, and seek the shelter of the Evil One.

The source of error is to disbelieve in the one true God, rely upon aught else but Him, and flee from His Decree.

True loss is for him whose days have been spent in utter ignorance of his true self.

The essence of all that We have revealed for thee is Justice, is for man to free himself from idle fancy and imitation, discern with the eye of oneness His glorious handiwork, and look into all things with a searching eye.

Thus have We instructed thee, manifested unto thee words of wisdom, that thou mayst be thankful unto the Lord, thy God, and glory therein amidst all peoples.

‘ABDU’L-BAHÁ

THE POWER OF THOUGHT

THE reality of man is his thought, not his material body. The thought force and the animal force are partners. Although man is part of the animal creation, he possesses a power of thought superior to all other created beings.

If a man's thought is constantly aspiring towards heavenly subjects then does he become saintly; if on the other hand his thought does not soar, but is directed downwards to center itself upon the things of this world, he grows more and more material until he arrives at a state little better than that of a mere animal.

Thoughts may be divided into two classes:—

Thought that belongs to the world of thought alone.

Thought that expresses itself in action.

Some men and women glory in their exalted thoughts, but, if these thoughts never reach the plane of action they remain useless: the power of thought is dependent on its manifestation in deeds. A philosopher's thought may, however, in the world of progress and evolution, translate itself into the actions of other people, even when he himself is unable or unwilling to show forth his grand ideals in his own life. To this class the majority of philosophers belong, their teachings being high above their actions. This is the difference between philosophers who are spiritual teachers, and those who are mere philosophers: the spiritual teacher is the first to follow his own teaching; he brings down into the world of action his spiritual conceptions and ideals. His divine thoughts are made manifest to the world. His thought is (a part of) himself, from which he is inseparable. When we find a philosopher emphasising the importance and grandeur of justice, and then encouraging a rapacious monarch in his oppression and tyranny, we quickly realize that he belongs to the first class: for he thinks heavenly thoughts and does not practise the corresponding heavenly virtues.

This state is impossible with spiritual philosophers, for they ever express their high and noble thoughts in actions.

Wisdom of 'Abdu'l-Bahá.

UNDERSTANDING

GOD'S greatest gift to man is that of intellect, or understanding.

The understanding is the power by which man acquires his knowledge of the several kingdoms of creation, and of various stages of existence, as well as of much which is invisible.

Possessing this gift, he is, in himself, the sum of earlier creations—he is able to get into touch with those kingdoms; and by this gift, he can frequently, through his scientific knowledge, reach out with prophetic vision.

Intellect is, in truth, the most precious gift bestowed upon man by the divine bounty. Man alone, among created beings, has this wonderful power.

All creation, preceding man, is bound by the stern law of nature. The great sun, the multitudes of stars, the oceans and seas, the mountains, the rivers, the trees, and all animals, great or small—none are able to evade obedience to nature's law.

Man alone has freedom, and, by his understanding or intellect, has been able to gain control of and adapt some of those natural laws to his own needs. By the power of his intellect he has discovered means by which he not only traverses great continents in express trains and crosses vast oceans in ships, but, like the fish, he travels under water in submarines, and, imitating the birds, he flies through the air in airships.

Man has succeeded in using electricity in several ways—for light, for motive power, for sending messages from one end of the earth to the other—and by electricity he can even hear a voice many miles away.

By this gift of understanding or intellect he has also been able to use the rays of the sun to picture people and things, and even to capture the form of distant heavenly bodies.

We perceive in what numerous ways man has been able to bend the powers of nature to his will.

How grievous it is to see how man has used his God-given gift to frame instruments of war, for breaking the commandment of God "Thou shalt not kill," and for defying Christ's injunction to "Love one another."

God gave this power to man that it might be used for the advancement of civilization, for the good of humanity, to increase love and concord and peace. But man prefers to use this gift to destroy instead of to build, for injustice and oppression, for hatred and discord and devastation, for the destruction of his fellow-creatures, whom Christ has commanded that he should love as himself!

I hope that you will use *your* understanding to promote the unity and tranquillity of mankind, to give enlightenment and civilization to the people, to produce love in all around you, and to bring about the Universal Peace.

Study the sciences, acquire more and more knowledge. Assuredly one may learn to the end of one's life! Use your knowledge always for the benefit of others; so may war cease from off the face of this beautiful earth, and a glorious edifice of peace and concord be raised. Strive that your high ideals may be realized in the Kingdom of God on earth, as they will be in heaven.

Wisdom of 'Abdu'l-Bahá.

The Three Degrees of Reality

THERE are in the world of humanity three degrees; those of the body, the soul, and spirit.

The body is the physical or animal degree of man. From the bodily point of view man is a sharer of the animal kingdom. The bodies alike of men and animals are composed of elements held together by the law of attraction.

Like the animal, man possesses the faculties of the senses, is subject to heat, cold, hunger, thirst, etc.; unlike the animal, man has a rational soul, the human intelligence.

This intelligence of man is the intermediary between his body and his spirit.

When man allows the spirit, through his soul, to

enlighten his understanding, then does he contain all creation; because man, being the culmination of all that went before and thus superior to all previous evolutions, contains all the lower world within himself. Illumined by the spirit through the instrumentality of the soul, man's radiant intelligence makes him the crowning-point of creation.

But on the other hand, when man does not open his mind and heart to the blessing of the spirit, but turns his soul towards the material side, towards the bodily part of his nature, then is he fallen from his high place and he becomes inferior to the inhabitants of the lower animal kingdom. In this case the man is in a sorry plight! For if the spiritual qualities of the soul, open to the breath of the divine spirit, are never used, they become atrophied, enfeebled, and at last incapable; whilst the soul's material qualities alone being exercised, they become terribly powerful—and the unhappy, misguided man becomes more savage, more unjust, more vile, more cruel, more malevolent than the lower animals themselves. All his aspirations and desires being strengthened by the lower side of the soul's nature, he becomes more and more brutal, until his whole being is in no way superior to that of the beasts that perish. Men such as this, plan to work evil, to hurt and to destroy; they are entirely without the spirit of divine compassion, for the celestial quality of the soul has been dominated by that of the material. If, on the contrary, the spiritual nature of the soul has been so strengthened that it holds the material side in subjection, then does the man approach the divine; his humanity becomes so glorified that the virtues of the celestial assembly are manifested in him; he radiates the mercy of God, he stimulates the spiritual progress of mankind, for he becomes a lamp to show light on their path.

You perceive how the soul is the intermediary between the body and the spirit. In like manner is this tree the intermediary between the seed and the fruit. When the fruit of the tree appears and becomes ripe, then we know that the tree is perfect; if the tree bore no fruit it would be merely a useless growth, serving no purpose.

When a soul has in it the life of the spirit, then does it bring forth good fruit and become a divine tree. I wish you to try to understand this example. I hope that the unspeakable goodness of God will so strengthen you that the celestial quality of your soul, which relates it to the spirit, will for ever dominate the material side, so entirely ruling the senses that your soul will approach the perfection of the heavenly Kingdom. May your faces, being steadfastly set towards the divine light, become so luminous that all your thoughts, words and actions will shine with the spiritual radiance dominating your souls, so that in the gatherings of the world you will show perfection in your life.

Some men's lives are solely occupied with the things of this world; their minds are so circumscribed by exterior manners and traditional interests that they are blind to any other realm of existence, to the spiritual significance of all things. They think and dream of earthly fame, of material progress. Sensuous delights and comfortable surroundings bound their horizon, their highest ambitions center in successes of worldly conditions and circumstances. They curb not their lower propensities; they eat, drink, and sleep. Like the animal, they have no thought beyond their own physical well-being. It is true that these necessities must be despatched. Life is a load which must be carried on while we are on earth, but the cares of the lower things of life should not be allowed to monopolize all the thoughts and aspirations of a human being. The heart's ambitions should ascend to a more glorious goal, mental activity should rise to higher levels. Men should hold in their souls the vision of celestial perfection, and there prepare a dwelling-place for the inexhaustible bounty of the divine spirit.

Let your ambition be the achievement on earth of a heavenly civilization! I ask for you the supreme blessing, that you may be so filled with the vitality of the heavenly spirit that you may be the cause of life to the world.

Wisdom of 'Abdu'l-Bahá.

Soul, Mind and Spirit

SOME one desires an explanation of the terms soul, mind and spirit. The terminology of ancient and modern philosophers differs. According to the great ancient philosophers the words soul, mind and spirit implied the underlying principles of life; the essence was expressed under different names, and these three terms designated the various functions of the absolute reality, or the operations of the one single essence; for instance, when they dealt with the sensation of emotion they called it the soul; when they desired to express that power which discovers the reality of phenomena they gave it the appellation of mind and when they discussed the consciousness which pervades the world of creation they gave it the title of spirit.

A man sees, hears, or speaks—seeing, hearing and speaking being the different functions of the same power or reality which animates him; the eye being the organ of sight, the ear of hearing and the tongue of speech. The one invisible primal essence had various names, but this in brief is the synopsis of the ancient philosophy.

We make a differentiation in these subjects. When we speak of the soul we mean the motive power of this physical body which lives under its entire control in accordance with its dictates. If the soul identifies itself with the material world it remains dark, for in the natural world there is corruption, aggression, struggles for existence, greed, darkness, transgression and vice. If the soul remains in this station and moves along these paths it will be the recipient of this darkness; but if it becomes the recipient of the graces of the world of mind, its darkness will be transformed into light, its tyranny into justice, its ignorance into wisdom, its aggression into loving kindness, until it reach the apex. Then there will not remain any struggle for existence. Man will become free from egotism; he will be released from the material world; he will become the personification of justice and virtue, for a sanctified soul illumines humanity and is an honor to mankind, conferring life upon the children of men and suffering all nations to attain to the station of perfect unity. Therefore, we can apply the name "holy soul" to such a one.

There is, however, a faculty in man which unfolds to his vision the secrets of existence. It gives him a power whereby he may investigate the reality of every object. It leads man on and on to the luminous station of divine sublimity and frees him from all the fetters of self, causing him to ascend to the pure heaven of sanctity. This is the power of the mind, for the soul is not, of itself, capable of unrolling the mysteries of phenomena; but the mind can accomplish this and therefore it is a power superior to the soul.

There is still another power which is differentiated from that of the soul and mind. This third power is the spirit which is an emanation from the divine Bestower; it is the effulgence of the sun of reality, the radiation of the celestial world, the spirit of faith, the spirit His Holiness the Christ refers to when he says, "Those that are born of the flesh are flesh, and those that are born of the spirit are spirit." The spirit is the axis round which the eternal life revolves. It is conducive to everlasting glory and is the cause of the exaltation of humanity.

In another instance His Holiness the Christ says, "Whosoever has not received a portion of the spirit is as dead. Let the dead bury their dead." This means that although the souls of humanity are living, yet if they are deprived of contact with the spirit they are as dead. In another place Christ says, "You must be baptized with the spirit." This spirit of faith is the flame of reality, the life of humanity and the cause of eternal illumination. It inspires man to attain the virtues and perfections of the divine world.

It is my hope that each one of you may become conscious of this flame.

Divine Philosophy.

NATURE

ABSOLUTE repose does not exist in nature. All things either make progress or lose ground. Everything moves forward or backward, nothing is without motion. From his birth, a man progresses physically until he reaches maturity, then, having arrived at the prime of his life, he begins to decline, the strength and powers of his body decrease, and he gradually arrives at the hour of death. Likewise a plant progresses from the seed to maturity, then its life begins to lessen until it fades and dies. A bird soars to a certain height and having reached the highest possible point in its flight, begins its descent to earth.

Thus it is evident that movement is essential to all existence. All material things progress to a certain point, then begin to decline. This is the law which governs the whole physical creation.

Now let us consider the soul. We have seen that movement is essential to existence; nothing that has life is without motion. All creation, whether of the mineral, vegetable or animal kingdom, is compelled to obey the law of motion; it must either ascend or descend. But with the human soul, there is no decline. Its only movement is towards perfection; growth and progress alone constitute the motion of the soul.

Divine perfection is infinite, therefore the progress of the soul is also infinite. From the very birth of a human being the soul progresses, the intellect grows and knowledge increases. When the body dies the soul lives on. All the differing degrees of created physical beings are limited, but the soul is limitless.

In all religions the belief exists that the soul survives the death of the body. Intercessions are sent up for the beloved dead, prayers are said for their progress and for the forgiveness of their sins. If the soul perished with the body all this would have no meaning. Further, if it were not possible for the soul to advance towards perfection after it had been released from the body, of what avail are all these loving prayers of devotion?

We read in the sacred writings that "all good works are found again." [1] Now, if the soul did not survive, this also would mean nothing.

The very fact that our spiritual instinct, surely never given in vain, prompts us to pray for the welfare of those, our loved ones, who have passed out of the material world: does it not bear witness to the continuance of their existence?

In the world of spirit there is no retrogression. The world of mortality is a world of contradictions, of opposites; motion being compulsory everything must either go forward or retreat. In the realm of spirit there is no retreat possible, all movement is bound to be towards a perfect state. "Progress" is the expression of spirit in the world of matter. The intelligence of man, his reasoning powers, his knowledge, his scientific achievements, all these, being manifestations of the spirit, partake of the inevitable law of spiritual progress and are, therefore, of necessity, immortal.

My hope for you is that you will progress in the world of spirit, as well as in the world of matter; that your intelligence will develop, your knowledge will augment, and your understanding be widened.

[1] i.e.—All good actions bring their own reward.

You must ever press forward, never standing still; avoid stagnation, the first step to a backward movement, to decay.

The whole physical creation is perishable. These material bodies are composed of atoms; when these atoms begin to separate decomposition sets in, then comes what we call death. This composition of atoms, which constitutes the body or mortal element of any created being, is temporary. When the power of attraction, which holds these atoms together, is withdrawn, the body, as such, ceases to exist.

With the soul it is different. The soul is not a combination of elements, it is not composed of many atoms, it is of one indivisible substance and therefore eternal. It is entirely out of the order of the physical creation; it is immortal.

Scientific philosophy has demonstrated that a *simple* element ("simple," meaning "not composed") is indestructible, eternal. The soul, not being a composition of elements, is, in character, as a simple element, and therefore cannot cease to exist.

The soul, being of that one indivisible substance, can suffer neither disintegration nor destruction, therefore there is no reason for its coming to an end. All things living show signs of their existence, and it follows that these signs could not of themselves exist if that which they express or to which they testify had no being. A thing which does not exist, can, of course, give no sign of its existence. The manifold signs of the existence of the spirit are for ever before us.

The traces of the spirit of Jesus Christ, the influence of his divine teaching, is present with us today, and is everlasting.

A non-existent thing, it is agreed, cannot be seen by signs. In order to write a man must exist—one who does not exist cannot write. Writing is, in itself, a sign of the writer's soul and intelligence. The Sacred Writings (with ever the same teaching) prove the continuity of the spirit.

Consider the aim of creation: is it possible that all is created to evolve and develop through countless ages with this small goal in view—a few years of a man's life on earth? Is it not unthinkable that this should be the final aim of existence?

The mineral evolves till it is absorbed in the life of the plant, the plant progresses till finally it loses its life in that of the animal; the animal, in its turn, forming part of the food of man, is absorbed into human life.

Thus, man is shown to be the sum of all creation, the superior of all created beings, the goal to which countless ages of existence have progressed.

At the best, man spends four-score years and ten in this world—a short time indeed!

Does a man cease to exist when he leaves the body? If his life comes to an end, then all the previous evolution is useless, all has been for nothing. Can one imagine that creation has no greater aim than this?

The soul is eternal, immortal.

Materialists say, "Where is the soul? What is it? We cannot see it, neither can we touch it."

This is how we must answer them:—However much the mineral may progress, it cannot comprehend the vegetable world. Now, that lack of comprehension does not prove the non-existence of the plant.

To however great a degree the plant may have evolved, it is unable to understand the animal world;

this ignorance is no proof that the animal does not exist.

The animal, be he ever so highly developed, cannot imagine the intelligence of man, neither can he realize the nature of his soul. But, again, this does not prove that man is without intellect, or without soul. It only demonstrates this, that one form of existence is incapable of comprehending a form superior to itself.

This flower may be unconscious of such a being as man, but the fact of its ignorance does not prevent the existence of humanity.

In the same way, if materialists do not believe in the existence of the soul, their unbelief does not prove that there is no such realm as the world of spirit. The very existence of man's intelligence proves his immortality; moreover, darkness proves the presence of light, for without light there would be no shadow. Poverty proves the existence of riches, for, without riches, how could we measure poverty? Ignorance proves that knowledge exists, for without knowledge how could there be ignorance?

Therefore the idea of mortality presupposes the existence of immortality—for if there were no life eternal, there would be no way of measuring the life of this world.

If the spirit were not immortal, how could the Manifestations of God endure such terrible trials?

Why did Christ Jesus suffer the fearful death on the cross?

Why did Muḥammad bear persecutions?

Why did the Báb make the supreme sacrifice and why did Bahá'u'lláh pass the years of his life in prison?

Why should all this suffering have been, if not to prove the everlasting life of the spirit?

Christ suffered, he accepted all his trials because of the immortality of his spirit. If a man reflects he will understand the spiritual significance of the law of progress; how all moves from the inferior to the superior degree.

It is only a man without intelligence who, after considering these things, can imagine that the great scheme of creation should suddenly cease to progress, that evolution should come to such an inadequate end!

Materialists who reason in this way, and contend that we are unable to *see* the world of spirit, or to perceive the blessings of God, are surely like the animals who have no understanding; having eyes they see not, ears they have, but do not hear. And this lack of sight and hearing is a proof of nothing but their own inferiority; of whom we read in the Qu'rán, "They are men who are blind and deaf to the spirit." They do not use that great gift of God, the power of the understanding, by which they might see with the eyes of the spirit, hear with spiritual ears and also comprehend with a divinely enlightened heart.

The inability of the materialistic mind to grasp the idea of the life eternal is no proof of the non-existence of that life.

The comprehension of that other life depends on our spiritual birth.

My prayer for you is that your spiritual faculties and aspirations may daily increase, and that you will never allow the material senses to veil from your eyes the glories of the heavenly illumination.

Wisdom of 'Abdu'l-Bahá.

Natural and Spiritual Man

IN man there are two natures; his spiritual or higher
nature and his material or lower nature. In one he
approaches God, in the other he lives for the world
alone. Signs of both these natures are to be found in
men. In his material aspect he expresses untruth,
cruelty and injustice; all these are the outcome of his
lower nature. The attributes of his divine nature are
shown forth in love, mercy, kindness, truth and justice, one and all being expressions of his higher
nature. Every good habit, every noble quality belongs to man's spiritual nature, whereas all his imperfections and sinful actions are born of his material
nature. If a man's divine nature dominates his human
nature, we have a saint.

Man has the power both to do good and to do evil;
if his power for good predominates and his inclina-
tions to do wrong are conquered, then man in truth
may be called a saint. But if, on the contrary, he
rejects the things of God and allows his evil passions
to conquer him, then he is no better than a mere
animal.

Saints are men who have freed themselves from the
world of matter and who have overcome sin. They
live in the world but are not of it, their thoughts
being continually in the world of the spirit. Their
lives are spent in holiness, and their deeds show forth
love, justice and godliness. They are illumined from
on high; they are as bright and shining lamps in the
dark places of the earth. These are the saints of God.
The apostles, who were the disciples of Jesus Christ,
were just as other men are; they, like their fellows,

were attracted by the things of the world, and each thought only of his own advantage. They knew little of justice, nor were the divine perfections found in their midst. But when they followed Christ and believed in him, their ignorance gave place to understanding, cruelty was changed to justice, falsehood to truth, darkness into light. They had been worldly, they became spiritual and divine. They had been children of darkness, they became sons of God, they became saints. Strive therefore to follow in their steps, leaving all worldly things behind, and striving to attain to the spiritual kingdom.

Pray to God that He may strengthen you in divine virtue, so that you may be as angels in the world, and beacons of light to disclose the mysteries of the Kingdom to those with understanding hearts.

God sent His prophets into the world to teach and enlighten man, to explain to him the mystery of the power of the Holy Spirit, to enable him to reflect the light, and so, in his turn, to be the source of guidance to others. The Heavenly Books, the Bible, the Qu'rán, and the other holy writings have been given by God as guides into the paths of divine virtue, love, justice and peace.

Therefore I say unto you that you should strive to follow the counsels of these blessed Books, and so order your lives that you may, following the examples set before you, become yourselves the saints of the Most High!

Wisdom of 'Abdu'l-Bahá.

EVOLUTION OF THE SOUL

GOD, in His bounty, has given us a foretaste here, has given us certain proofs of the difference that exists between body, soul and spirit.

We see that cold, heat, suffering, etc., only concern the *body*, they do not touch the spirit.

How often do we see a man poor, sick, miserably clad, and with no means of support, yet spiritually strong. Whatever his body has to suffer, his spirit is free and well. Again, how often do we see a rich man, physically strong and healthy, but with a soul sick unto death.

It is quite apparent to the seeing mind that a man's spirit is something very different to his physical body.

The spirit is changeless, indestructible. The progress and development of the soul, the joy and sorrow of the soul, are independent of the physical body.

If we are caused joy or pain by a friend, if a love prove true or false, it is the soul that is affected. If our dear ones are far from us—it is the soul that grieves, and the grief or trouble of the soul may react on the body.

Thus, when the spirit is fed with holy virtues, then is the body joyous; if the soul falls into sin, the body is in torment.

When we find truth, constancy, fidelity and love, we are happy; but if we meet with lying, faithlessness and deceit, we are miserable.

These are all things pertaining to the soul, and are not *bodily* ills. Thus, it is apparent that the soul, even as the body, has its own individuality. But if the body undergoes a change, the spirit need not be touched.

When you break a glass on which the sun shines, the glass is broken, but the sun still shines. If a cage containing a bird is destroyed, the bird is unharmed. If a lamp is broken, the flame can still burn bright.

The same thing applies to the spirit of man. Though death destroy his body, it has no power over his spirit—this is eternal, everlasting, both birthless and deathless.

As to the soul of man after death, it remains in the degree of purity to which it has evolved during life in the physical body, and after it is freed from the body it remains plunged in the ocean of God's mercy.

From the moment the soul leaves the body and arrives in the heavenly world, its evolution is spiritual, and that evolution is: *The approaching unto* God.

In the physical creation, evolution is from one degree of perfection to another. The mineral passes with its mineral perfections to the vegetable; the vegetable, with its perfection, passes to the animal world, and so on to that of humanity. This world is full of seeming contradictions; in each of these kingdoms (mineral, vegetable and animal) life exists in its degree; though, when compared to the life in a man, the earth appears to be dead, yet she, too, lives and has a life of her own. In this world things live and die, and live again in other forms of life, but in the world of the spirit it is quite otherwise.

The soul does not evolve from degree to degree as a law—it only evolves nearer to God, by the mercy and bounty of God.

Try with all your hearts to be willing channels for God's bounty. For I say unto you that He has chosen you to be His messengers of love throughout the world, to be His bearers of spiritual gifts to man, to be the means of spreading unity and concord on the earth. Thank God with all your hearts that such a privilege has been given unto you. For a life devoted to praise is not too long in which to thank God for such a favor.

Lift up your hearts above the present and look with eyes of faith into the future! Today the seed is sown, the grain falls upon the earth, but behold the day will come when it shall rise a glorious tree and the branches thereof shall be laden with fruit. Rejoice and be glad that this day has dawned, try to realize its power, for it is indeed wonderful! God has crowned you with honor and in your hearts has He set a radiant star; verily the light thereof shall brighten the whole world.

Wisdom of 'Abdu'l-Bahá.

IMMORTALITY

ACCORDING to divine philosophy, there are two important and universal conditions in the world of material phenomena; one which concerns life, the other concerning death; one relative to existence, the other non-existence; one manifest in composition, the other in decomposition. Some define existence as the expression of reality or being, and non-existence as non-being, imagining that death is annihilation. This is a mistaken idea, for total annihilation is an impossibility. At most, composition is ever subject to decomposition or disintegration; that is to say, exist-ence implies the grouping of material elements in a form or body, and non-existence is simply the decomposing of these groupings. This is the law of creation in its endless forms and infinite variety of expression. Certain elements have formed the composite creature man. This composite association of the elements in the form of a human body is therefore subject to disintegration which we call death, but after disintegration the elements themselves persist unchanged. Therefore total annihilation is an impossibility, and existence can never become non-existence. This would be equivalent to saying that light can become darkness, which is manifestly untrue and impossible. As existence can never become non-existence, there is no death for man; nay, rather, man is everlasting and everliving. The rational proof of this is that the atoms of the material elements are transferable from one form of existence to another, from one degree and kingdom to another, lower or higher. For example, an atom of the soil or dust of earth may traverse the kingdoms from mineral to man by successive incorporations into the bodies of the organisms of those kingdoms. At one time it enters into the formation of the mineral or rock; it is then absorbed by the vegetable kingdom and becomes a constituent of the body and fibre of a tree; again it is appropriated by the animal, and at a still later period is found in the body of man. Throughout these degrees of its traversing the kingdoms from one form of phenomenal being to another, it retains its atomic existence and is never annihilated nor relegated to non-existence.

Non-existence therefore is an expression applied to change of form, but this transformation can never be rightly considered annihilation, for the elements of composition are ever present and existent as we have seen in the journey of the atom through successive kingdoms, unimpaired; hence there is no death; life is everlasting. So to speak, when the atom entered into the composition of the tree, it died to the mineral kingdom, and when consumed by the animal, it died to the vegetable kingdom, and so on until its transference or transmutation into the kingdom of man; but throughout its traversing it was subject to transformation and not annihilation. Death therefore is applicable to change or transference from one degree or condition to another. In the mineral realm there was a spirit of existence; in the world of plant life and organisms it reappeared as the vegetative spirit; thence it attained the animal spirit and finally aspired to the human spirit. These are degrees and changes but not obliteration; and this is a rational proof that man is everlasting; ever living. Therefore death is only a relative term implying change. For example, we will say that this light before me, having reappeared in another incandescent lamp, has died in the one and lives in the other. This is not death in reality. The perfections of the mineral are translated into the vegetable and from thence into the animal, the virtue always attaining a plus or superlative degree in the upward change. In each kingdom we find the same virtues manifesting themselves more fully, proving that the reality has been transferred from a lower to a higher form and kingdom of being. Therefore nonexistence is only relative and absolute non-existence inconceivable. This rose in my hand will become disintegrated and its symmetry destroyed, but the elements of its composition remain changeless; nothing affects their elemental integrity. They cannot become non-existent; they are simply transferred from one state to another.

Through his ignorance, man fears death; but the death he shrinks from is imaginary and absolutely unreal; it is only human imagination.

The bestowal and grace of God have quickened the realm of existence with life and being. For existence there is neither change nor transformation; existence is ever existence; it can never be translated into non-existence. It is gradation; a degree below a higher degree is considered as non-existence. This dust beneath our feet, as compared with our being, is non-existent. When the human body crumbles into dust we can say it has become non-existent; therefore its dust in relation to living forms of human being is as non-existent but in its own sphere it is existent, it has its mineral being. Therefore it is well proved that absolute non-existence is impossible; it is only relative.

The purpose is this;—that the everlasting bestowal of God vouchsafed to man is never subject to corruption. Inasmuch as He has endowed the phenomenal world with being, it is impossible for that world to become non-being, for it is the very genesis of God; it is in the realm of origination; it is a creational and not a subjective world, and the bounty descending upon it is continuous and permanent. Therefore man the highest creature of the phenomenal world is endowed with that continuous bounty bestowed by divine generosity without cessation. For instance, the rays of the sun are continuous, the heat of the sun emanates from it without cessation; no discontinuance of it is conceivable. Even so the bestowal of God is descending upon the world of humanity, never ceasing, continuous, forever. If we say that the bestowal of existence ceases or falters it is equivalent to saying that the sun can exist with cessation of its effulgence. Is this possible? Therefore the effulgences of existence are ever-present and continuous.

The conception of annihilation is a factor in human degradation, a cause of human debasement and lowliness, a source of human fear and abjection. It has been conducive to the dispersion and weakening of human thought whereas the realization of existence and continuity has upraised man to sublimity of ideals, established the foundations of human progress and stimulated the development of heavenly virtues; therefore it behooves man to abandon thoughts of non-existence and death which are absolutely imaginary and see himself ever living, everlasting in the divine purpose of his creation. He must turn away from ideas which degrade the human soul, so that day by day and hour by hour he may advance upward and higher to spiritual perception of the continuity of the human reality. If he dwells upon the thought of non-existence he will become utterly incompetent; with weakened will-power his ambition for progress will be lessened and the acquisition of human virtues will cease.

Therefore you must thank God that He has bestowed upon you the blessing of life and existence in the human kingdom. Strive diligently to acquire virtues befitting your degree and station. Be as lights of the world which cannot be hid and which have no setting in horizons of darkness. Ascend to the zenith of an existence which is never beclouded by the fears and forebodings of non-existence. When man is not endowed with inner perception he is not informed of these important mysteries. The retina

of outer vision though sensitive and delicate may
nevertheless be a hindrance to the inner eye which
alone can perceive. The bestowals of God which are
manifest in all phenomenal life are sometimes hidden
by intervening veils of mental and mortal vision
which render man spiritually blind and incapable but
when those scales are removed and the veils rent
asunder, then the great signs of God will become
visible and he will witness the eternal light filling the
world. The bestowals of God are always manifest.
The promises of heaven are ever present. The favors
of God are all-surrounding but should the conscious
eye of the soul of man remain veiled and darkened
he will be led to deny these universal signs and remain
deprived of these manifestations of divine bounty.
Therefore we must endeavor with heart and soul in
order that the veil covering the eye of inner vision
may be removed, that we may behold the manifestations of the signs of God, discern His mysterious
graces, and realize that material blessings as compared
with spiritual bounties are as nothing. The spiritual
blessings of God are greatest. When we were in the
mineral kingdom, although endowed with certain
gifts and powers, they were not to be compared with
the blessings of the human kingdom. In the matrix
of the mother we were the recipients of endowments
and blessings of God, yet these were as nothing compared to the powers and graces bestowed upon us
after birth into this human world. Likewise if we
are born from the matrix of this physical and phenomenal environment into the freedom and loftiness
of the life and vision spiritual, we shall consider this
mortal existence and its blessings as worthless by
comparison.

In the spiritual world, the divine bestowals are infinite, for in that realm there is neither separation nor disintegration which characterize the world of material existence. Spiritual existence is absolute immortality, completeness and unchangeable being. Therefore we must thank God that He has created for us both material blessings and spiritual bestowals. He has given us material gifts and spiritual graces, outer sight to view the lights of the sun and inner vision by which we may perceive the glory of God. He has designed the outer ear to enjoy the melodies of sound and the inner hearing wherewith we may hear the voice of our Creator. We must strive with energies of heart, soul and mind to develop and manifest the perfections and virtues latent within the realities of the phenomenal world, for the human reality may be compared to a seed. If we sow the seed, a mighty tree appears from it. The virtues of the seed are revealed in the tree; it puts forth branches, leaves, blossoms, and produces fruit. All these virtues were hidden and potential in the seed. Through the blessing and bounty of cultivation these virtues became apparent. Similarly the merciful God our Creator has deposited within human realities certain virtues latent and potential. Through education and culture, these virtues deposited by the loving God will become apparent in the human reality even as the unfoldment of the tree from within the germinating seed.

Promulgation of Universal Peace.

THE DIVINE SPIRIT

THE greatest power in the realm and range of human existence is spirit—the divine breath which animates and pervades all things. It is manifested throughout creation in different degrees or kingdoms. In the vegetable kingdom it is the spirit augmentative or power of growth, the animus of life and development in plants, trees and organisms of the floral world. In this degree of its manifestation, spirit is unconscious of the powers which qualify the kingdom of the animal. The distinctive virtue or plus of the animal is sense perception; it sees, hears, smells, tastes and feels but is incapable in turn, of conscious ideation or reflection which characterize and differentiate the human kingdom. The animal neither exercises nor apprehends this distinctive human power and gift. From the visible it cannot draw conclusions regarding the invisible whereas the human mind from visible and known premises attains knowledge of the unknown and invisible. For instance, Christopher Columbus from information based upon known and provable facts drew conclusions which led him unerringly across the vast ocean to the unknown continent of America. Such power of accomplishment is beyond the range of animal intelligence. Therefore this power is a distinctive attribute of the human spirit and kingdom. The animal spirit cannot penetrate and discover the mysteries of things. It is a captive of the senses. No amount of teaching, for instance, would enable it to grasp the fact that the sun is stationary and the earth moves around it. Likewise the human spirit has its limitations.   It cannot comprehend the phenomena of the kingdom transcending the human station, for it is a captive of powers and life forces which have their operation upon its own plane of existence and it cannot go beyond that boundary.

There is however another spirit which may be termed the divine, to which Jesus Christ refers when he declares that man must be born of its quickening and baptized with its living fire. Souls deprived of that spirit are accounted as dead, though they are possessed of the human spirit. His Holiness Jesus Christ has pronounced them dead inasmuch as they have no portion of the divine spirit. He says "Let the dead bury their dead." In another instance he declares, "That which is born of the flesh is flesh; and that which is born of the spirit is spirit." By this he means that souls though alive in the human kingdom are nevertheless dead if devoid of this particular spirit of divine quickening. They have not partaken of the divine life of the higher kingdom; for the soul which partakes of the power of the divine spirit is verily living.

This quickening spirit has spontaneous emanation from the Sun of Truth, from the reality of divinity and is not a revelation or a manifestation. It is like the rays of the sun. The rays are emanations from the sun. This does not mean that the sun has become divisible; that a part of the sun has come out into space. This plant beside me has risen from the seed; therefore it is a manifestation and unfoldment of the seed. The seed, as you can see, has unfolded in manifestation and the result is this plant. Every leaf of the plant is a part of the seed. But the reality of divinity is indivisible and each individual of human kind cannot be a part of it as is often claimed. Nay, rather, the individual realities of mankind when spiritually born are emanations from the reality of divinity, just as the flame, heat and light of the sun are the effulgence of the sun and not a part of the sun itself. Therefore a spirit has emanated from the reality of divinity, and its effulgences have become visible in human entities or realities. This ray and this heat are permanent. There is no cessation in the effulgence. As long as the sun exists the heat and light will exist, and inasmuch as eternality is a property of divinity, this emanation is everlasting. There is no cessation in its outpouring. The more the world of humanity develops, the more the effulgences or emanations of divinity will become revealed, just as the stone when it becomes polished and pure as a mirror will reflect in fuller degree the glory and splendor of the sun.

The mission of the prophets, the revelation of the Holy Books, the manifestation of the heavenly teachers and the purpose of divine philosophy all center in the training of the human realities so that they may become clear and pure as mirrors and reflect the light and love of the Sun of Reality. Therefore I hope that whether you be in the east or the west you will strive with heart and soul in order that day by day the world of humanity may become glorified, more spiritual, more sanctified; and that the splendor of the Sun of Reality may be revealed fully in human hearts as in a mirror. This is worthy of the world of mankind. This is the true evolution and progress of humanity. This is the supreme bestowal. Otherwise, by simple development along material lines man is not perfected. At most, the physical aspect of man,

his natural or material conditions may become stabil-
ized and improved but he will remain deprived of the
spiritual or divine bestowal. He is then like a body
without a spirit, a lamp without the light, an eye
without the power of vision, an ear that hears no
sound, a mind incapable of perceiving, an intellect
minus the power of reason.

Man has two powers, and his development two
aspects. One power is connected with the material
world and by it he is capable of material advancement. The other power is spiritual and through its
development his inner, potential nature is awakened.
These powers are like two wings. Both must be developed, for flight is impossible with one wing. Praise
be to God! material advancement has been evident
in the world but there is need of spiritual advancement in like proportion. We must strive unceasingly
and without rest to accomplish the development of
the spiritual nature in man, and endeavor with tireless
energy to advance humanity toward the nobility of
its true and intended station. For the body of man is
accidental; it is of no importance. The time of its
disintegration will inevitably come. But the spirit of
man is essential and therefore eternal. It is a divine
bounty. It is the effulgence of the Sun of Reality and
therefore of greater importance than the physical
body.

Promulgation of Universal Peace.

Nature and the Word

NATURE is the material world. When we look upon it we see that it is dark and imperfect. For instance, if we allow a piece of land to remain in its natural condition, we will find it covered with thorns and thistles; useless weeds and wild vegetation will flourish upon it and it will become like a jungle. The trees will be fruitless, lacking beauty and symmetry; wild animals, noxious insects and reptiles will abound in its dark recesses. This is the incompleteness and imperfection of the world of nature. To change these conditions, we must clear the ground and cultivate it so that flowers may grow instead of thorns and weeds; that is to say, we must illumine the dark world of nature. In their primal natural state, the forests are dim, gloomy, impenetrable. Man opens them to the light, clears away the tangled underbrush and plants fruitful trees. Soon the wild woodlands and jungle are changed into productive orchards and beautiful gardens; order has replaced chaos; the dark realm of nature has become illumined and brightened by cultivation.

If man himself is left in his natural state, he will become lower than the animal and continue to grow more ignorant and imperfect. The savage tribes of Central Africa are evidences of this. Left in their natural condition, they have sunk to the lowest depths and degrees of barbarism, dimly groping in a world of mental and moral obscurity. If we wish to illumine this dark plane of human existence we must bring man forth from the hopeless captivity of nature, educate him and show him the pathway

of light and knowledge, until, uplifted from his condition of ignorance, he becomes wise and knowing;
no longer savage and revengeful, he becomes civilized
and kind; once evil and sinister, he is endowed with
the attributes of heaven. But left in his natal condition without education and training, it is certain
that he will become more depraved and vicious than
the animal, even to the extreme degree witnessed
among African tribes who practice cannibalism. It
is evident therefore that the world of nature is incomplete, imperfect until awakened and illumined by the
light and stimulus of education.

In these days there are new schools of philosophy
blindly claiming that the world of nature is perfect.
If this is true, why are children trained and educated
in schools, and what is the need of extended courses
in sciences, arts and letters in colleges and universities? What would be the result if humanity was left
in its natal condition without education or training?
All scientific discoveries and attainments are the outcome of knowledge and education. The telegraph,
phonograph, telephone were latent and potential in
the world of nature but would never have come forth
into the realm of visibility unless man through education had penetrated and discovered the laws which
control them. All the marvelous developments and
miracles of what we call civilization would have
remained hidden, unknown and so to speak, non-
existent, if man had remained in his natural condition,
deprived of the bounties, blessings and benefits of
education and mental culture. The intrinsic difference
between the ignorant man and the astute philosopher
is that the former has not been lifted out of his
natural condition, while the latter has undergone

systematic training and education in schools and colleges until his mind has awakened and unfolded to higher realms of thought and perception; otherwise both are human and natural.

God has sent forth the prophets for the purpose of quickening the soul of man into higher and divine recognitions. He has revealed the heavenly books for this great purpose. For this the breaths of the Holy Spirit have been wafted through the gardens of human hearts, the doors of the divine kingdom opened to mankind and the invisible inspirations sent forth from on high. This divine and ideal power has been bestowed upon man in order that he may purify himself from the imperfections of nature and uplift his soul to the realm of might and power. God has purposed that the darkness of the world of nature shall be dispelled and the imperfect attributes of the natal self be effaced in the effulgent reflection of the Sun of Truth. The mission of the prophets of God has been to train the souls of humanity and free them from the thraldom of natural instincts and physical tendencies. They are like unto gardeners, and the world of humanity is the field of their cultivation, the wilderness and untrained jungle growth wherein they proceed to labor. They cause the crooked branches to become straightened, the fruitless trees to become fruitful, and gradually transform this great wild uncultivated field into a beautiful orchard producing wonderful abundance and outcome.

If the world of nature was perfect and complete in itself, there would be no need of such training and cultivation in the human world; no need of teachers, schools and universities, arts and crafts. The revelations of the prophets of God would not have been

necessary and the heavenly books would have been
superfluous. If the world of nature was perfect and
sufficient for mankind we would have no need of
God and our belief in Him. Therefore the bestowal
of all these great helps and accessories to the attainment of divine life is because the world of nature is
incomplete and imperfect. Consider this Canadian
country during the early history of Montreal when
the land was in its wild, uncultivated and natural
condition. The soil was unproductive, rocky and
almost uninhabitable, vast forests stretching in every
direction. What invisible power caused this great
metropolis to spring up amid such savage and
forbidding conditions? It was the human mind.
Therefore nature and the effect of nature's laws were
imperfect. The mind of man remedied and removed
this imperfect condition, until now we behold a great
city instead of a savage unbroken wilderness. Before
the coming of Columbus, America itself was a wild,
uncultivated expanse of primeval forest, mountains
and rivers—a very world of nature. Now it has become the world of man. It was dark, forbidding and
savage; now it has become illumined with a great
civilization and prosperity. Instead of forests, we
behold productive farms, beautiful gardens and pro-
lific orchards. Instead of thorns and useless vegetation,
we find flowers, domestic animals and fields awaiting
harvest. If the world of nature was perfect, the condition of this great country would have been left
unchanged.

If a child is left in its natural state and deprived
of education, there is no doubt that it will grow
up in ignorance and illiteracy, its mental faculties
dulled and dimmed; in fact it will become like an

animal. This is evident among the savages of Central Africa who are scarcely higher than the beast in mental development.

The conclusion is irresistible that the splendors of the Sun of Truth, the Word of God have been the source and cause of human upbuilding and civilization. The world of nature is the kingdom of the animal. In its natural condition and plane of limitation the animal is perfect. The ferocious beasts of prey have been completely subject to the laws of nature in their development. They are without education or training; they have no power of abstract reasoning and intellectual ideals; they have no touch with the spiritual world and are without conception of God or the Holy Spirit. The animal can neither recognize nor apprehend the spiritual power of man, and makes no distinction between man and itself for the reason that its susceptibilities are limited to the plane of the senses. It lives under the bondage of nature and nature's laws. All the animals are materialists. They are deniers of God and without realization of a transcendent power in the universe. They have no knowledge of the divine prophets and holy books; mere captives of nature and the sense world. In reality they are like the great philosophers of this day who are not in touch with God and the Holy Spirit; deniers of the prophets, ignorant of spiritual susceptibilities, deprived of the heavenly bounties and without belief in the power supernatural. The animal lives this kind of life blissfully and untroubled whereas the material philosophers labor and study for ten or twenty years in schools and colleges, denying God, the Holy Spirit and divine inspirations. The animal is even a greater philosopher, for it attains the ability to do this without labor and study. For instance, the cow denies God and the Holy Spirit, knows nothing of divine inspirations, heavenly bounties or spiritual emotions and is a stranger to the world of hearts. Like the philosophers, the cow is a captive of nature and knows nothing beyond the range of the senses. The philosophers however glory in this saying, "We are not captives of superstitions; we have implicit faith in the impressions of the senses and know nothing beyond the realm of nature which contains and covers everything." But the cow without study or proficiency in the sciences, modestly and quietly views life from the same standpoint, living in harmony with nature's laws in the utmost dignity and nobility.

This is not the glory of man. The glory of man is in the knowledge of God, spiritual susceptibilities, attainment to transcendent powers and the bounties of the Holy Spirit. The glory of man is in being informed of the teachings of God. This is the glory of humanity. Ignorance is not glory but darkness. Can these souls who are steeped in the lower strata of ignorance become informed of the mysteries of God and the realities of existence yet His Holiness Jesus Christ be without knowledge of them? Is the intellect of these people greater than the intellect of Christ? His Holiness Christ was heavenly, divine and belonged to the world of the kingdom. He was the embodiment of spiritual knowledge. His intellect was superior to these philosophers, his comprehension deeper, his perception keener, his knowledge more perfect. How is it that he overlooked and denied himself everything in this world? He attached little importance to this material life, denying himself rest and composure, accepting trials and voluntarily suffering vicissitudes because he was endowed with spiritual susceptibilities and the power of the Holy Spirit. He beheld the splendors of the divine kingdom, embodied the bounties of God and possessed ideal powers. He was illumined with love and mercy and so likewise were all the prophets of God.

Promulgation of Universal Peace.

THE MEDIATOR

THE divine Reality is unthinkable, limitless, eternal, immortal and invisible.

The world of creation is bound by natural law, finite and mortal.

The infinite Reality cannot be said to ascend or descend. It is beyond the understanding of man, and cannot be described in terms which apply to the phenomenal sphere of the created world.

Man, then, is in extreme need of the only power by which he is able to receive help from the divine Reality, that power alone bringing him into contact with the source of all life.

An intermediary is needed to bring two extremes into relation with each other. Riches and poverty, plenty and need: without an intermediary power there could be no relation between these pairs of opposites.

So we can say that there must be a Mediator between God and man, and this is none other than the Holy Spirit, which brings the created earth into relation with the "Unthinkable One," the divine Reality.

The divine Reality may be likened to the sun and the Holy Spirit to the rays of the sun. As the rays of the sun bring the light and warmth of the sun to the earth, giving life to all created beings, so do the "Manifestations" bring the power of the Holy Spirit from the divine Sun of Reality to give light and life to the souls of men.

Behold, there is an intermediary necessary between the sun and the earth; the sun does not descend to the earth, neither does the earth ascend to the sun. This contact is made by the rays of the sun which bring light and warmth and heat.

The Holy Spirit is the light from the Sun of Truth bringing, by its infinite power, life and illumination to all mankind, flooding all souls with divine radiance, conveying the blessings of God's mercy to the whole world. The earth, without the medium of the warmth and light of the rays of the sun, could receive no benefits from the sun.

Likewise the Holy Spirit is the very cause of the life of man; without the Holy Spirit he would have no intellect, he would be unable to acquire his scientific knowledge by which his great influence over the rest of creation is gained. The illumination of the Holy Spirit gives to man the power of thought, and enables him to make discoveries by which he bends the laws of nature to his will.

The Holy Spirit it is which, through the mediation of the prophets of God, teaches spiritual virtues to man and enables him to attain eternal life.

All these blessings are brought to man by the Holy Spirit; therefore we can understand that the Holy

Spirit is the Intermediary between the creator and the created. The light and heat of the sun cause the earth to be fruitful, and create life in all things that grow; and the Holy Spirit quickens the souls of men.

The two great Apostles, St. Peter and St. John the Evangelist, were once simple, humble workmen, toiling for their daily bread. By the power of the Holy Spirit their souls were illumined, and they received the eternal blessings of Christ.

Wisdom of 'Abdu'l-Bahá.

THE MYSTERY OF SACRIFICE

THIS evening I wish to speak to you concerning the mystery of sacrifice. There are two kinds of sacrifice, the physical and the spiritual. The explanation made by the churches concerning this subject is in reality superstition. For instance it is recorded in the gospel that His Holiness Christ said, "I am the living bread which came down from heaven: if any man eat of this bread he shall live forever." He also said, "This wine is my blood which is shed for the remission of sins." These verses have been interpreted by the churches in such a superstitious way that it is impossible for human reason to understand or accept the explanation.

They say that His Holiness Adam disobeyed the command of God and partook of the fruit of the forbidden tree thereby committing a sin which was transmitted as a heritage to his posterity. They teach that because of Adam's sin all his descendants have likewise committed transgression and have become responsible through inheritance; consequently all mankind deserves punishment and must make retribution; and that God sent forth His son as a sacrifice in order that man might be forgiven and the human race delivered from the consequences of Adam's transgression.

We wish to consider these statements from the standpoint of reason. Could we conceive of His Highness the Divinity who is justice itself, inflicting punishment upon the posterity of Adam for Adam's own sin and disobedience? Even if we should see a governor, an earthly ruler punishing a son for the wrong-doing of his father, we would look upon that ruler as an unjust man. Granted the father committed a wrong, what was the wrong committed by the son? There is no connection between the two. Adam's sin was not the sin of his posterity especially as Adam is a thousand generations back of the man today. If the father of a thousand generations committed a sin, is it just to demand that the present generation should suffer the consequences thereof?

There are other questions and evidences to be considered. His Holiness Abraham was a manifestation of God and a descendant of Adam; likewise His Holiness Ishmael, His Holiness Isaac, His Holiness Jeremiah and the whole line of prophets including David, Solomon and Aaron were among his posterity. Were all these holy men condemned to a realm of punishment because of a deed committed by the first father, because of a mistake said to have been made by their mutual and remotest ancestor, His Holiness Adam? The explanation is made that when His Holiness Christ came and sacrificed himself, all the line of holy prophets who preceded him became free from sin and punishment. Even a child could not justly make such an assertion. These interpretations and statements are due to a misunderstanding of the meanings of the Bible.

In order to understand the reality of sacrifice let us consider the crucifixion and death of His Holiness Jesus Christ. It is true that he sacrificed himself for our sake. What is the meaning of this? When His Holiness Christ appeared, he knew that he must proclaim himself in opposition to all the nations and peoples of the earth. He knew that mankind would arise against him and inflict upon him all manner of tribulations. There is no doubt that one who put forth such a claim as Christ announced, would arouse the hostility of the world and be subjected to personal abuse. He realized that his blood would be shed and his body rent by violence. Notwithstanding his knowledge of what would befall him, he arose to proclaim his message, suffered all tribulation and hardships from the people and finally offered his life as a sacrifice in order to illumine humanity; gave his blood in order to guide the world of mankind. He accepted every calamity and suffering in order to guide men to the truth. Had he desired to save his own life and were he without wish to offer himself in sacrifice he would not have been able to guide a single soul. There was no doubt that his blessed blood would be shed and his body broken. Nevertheless that holy soul accepted calamity and death in his love for mankind. This is one of the meanings of sacrifice.

As to the second meaning, he said, "I am the bread which came down from heaven." It was not the body of Christ which came from heaven. His body came from the womb of Mary but the Christ perfections descended from heaven; the reality of Christ came down from heaven. The spirit of Christ and not the body descended from heaven. The body of Christ was but human. There could be no question that the physical body was born from the womb of Mary. But the reality of Christ, the spirit of Christ, the perfections of Christ all came from heaven. Consequently by saying he was the bread which came from heaven he meant that the perfections which he showed forth were divine perfections, that the blessings within him were heavenly gifts and bestowals, that his light was the light of reality. He said, "If any man eat of this bread, he shall live forever." That is to say whosoever assimilates these divine perfections which are within me will never die; whosoever has a share and partakes of these heavenly bounties I embody will find eternal life; he who takes unto himself these divine lights shall find life everlasting. How manifest the meaning is! How evident! For the soul which acquires divine perfections and seeks heavenly illumination from the teachings of Christ will undoubtedly live eternally. This is also one of the mysteries of sacrifice.

In reality His Holiness Abraham sacrificed himself, for he brought heavenly teachings to the world and conferred heavenly food upon mankind.

As to the third meaning of sacrifice, it is this:—If you plant a seed in the ground a tree will become manifest from that seed. The seed sacrifices itself to the tree that will come from it. The seed is outwardly lost, destroyed but the same seed which is sacrificed will be absorbed and embodied in the tree, its blossoms, fruit and branches. If the identity of that seed had not been sacrificed to the tree which became manifest from it, no branches, blossoms or fruits would have been forthcoming. His Holiness Christ outwardly disappeared. His personal identity became hidden from the eyes even as the identity of the seed disappeared, but the bounties, divine qualities and perfections of Christ became manifest in the Christion community which Christ founded through sacrificing himself. When you look at the tree you will realize that the perfections, blessings, properties and beauty of the seed have become manifest in the branches, twigs, blossoms and fruit; consequently the seed has sacrificed itself to the tree. Had it not done so, the tree would not have come into existence. His Holiness Christ like unto the seed sacrificed himself for the tree of Christianity. Therefore his perfections, bounties, favors, lights and graces became manifest in the Christian community, for the coming of which he sacrificed himself.

As to the fourth significance of sacrifice, it is the principle that a reality sacrifices its own characteristics. Man must sever himself from the influences of the world of matter, from the world of nature and its laws; for the material world is the world of corruption and death. It is the world of evil and darkness, of animalism and ferocity, bloodthirstiness, ambition and avarice, of self-worship, egotism and passion; it is the world of nature. Man must strip himself of all these imperfections, must sacrifice these tendencies which are peculiar to the outer and material world of existence.

On the other hand man must acquire heavenly qualities and attain divine attributes. He must become the image and likeness of God. He must seek the bounty of the eternal, become the manifester of the love of God, the light of guidance, the tree of life and the depository of the bounties of God. That is to say man must sacrifice the qualities and attributes of the world of nature for the qualities and attributes of the world of God. For instance consider the substance we call iron. Observe its qualities; it is solid, black, cold. These are the characteristics of iron. When the same iron absorbs heat from the fire, it sacrifices its attribute of solidity for the attribute of fluidity. It sacrifices its attribute of darkness for the attribute of light which is a quality of the fire. It sacrifices its attribute of coldness to the quality of heat which the fire possesses; so that in the iron there remains no solidity, darkness or cold. It becomes illumined and transformed having sacrificed its qualities to the qualities and attributes of the fire.

Likewise man when separated and severed from the attributes of the world of nature sacrifices the qualities and exigencies of that mortal realm and manifests the perfections of the Kingdom, just as the qualities of the iron disappeared and the qualities of the fire appeared in their place.

Every man trained through the teachings of God and illumined by the light of His guidance, who becomes a believer in God and His signs and is enkindled with the fire of the love of God sacrifices the imperfections of nature for the sake of divine perfections. Consequently every perfect person, every illumined, heavenly individual stands in the station of sacrifice. It is my hope that through the assistance and providence of God and through the bounties of the kingdom of Abhá you may be entirely severed from the imperfections of the world of nature, purified from selfish, human desires, receiving life from the kingdom of Abhá and attaining heavenly graces. May the divine light become manifest upon your faces, the fragrances of holiness refresh your nostrils and the breath of the Holy Spirit quicken you with eternal life.

Promulgation of Universal Peace.

SPIRITUAL TRUTH IS REVEALED

IT is a self-evident fact that phenomenal existence can never grasp nor comprehend the ancient and essential reality. Utter weakness cannot understand absolute strength. When we view the world of creation we discover differences in degree which make it impossible for the lower to comprehend the higher. For example, the mineral kingdom, no matter how much it may advance can never comprehend the phenomena of the vegetable kingdom. Whatever development the vegetable may attain, it can have no message from nor come in touch with the kingdom of the animal. However perfect may be the growth of a tree it cannot realize the sensation of sight, hearing, smell, taste and touch; these are beyond its limitation. Although it is the possessor of existence in the world of creation, a tree nevertheless has no knowledge of the superior degree of the animal kingdom. Likewise no matter how great the advancement of the animal it can have no idea of the human plane; no knowledge of intellect and spirit. Difference in degree is an obstacle to this comprehension. A lower degree cannot comprehend a higher although all are

in the same world of creation, whether mineral, vegetable or animal. Degree is the barrier and limitation.
In the human plane of existence we can say we have
knowledge of a vegetable, its qualities and product,
but the vegetable has no knowledge or comprehension
whatever of us. No matter how near perfection this
rose may advance in its own sphere it can never possess hearing and sight. Inasmuch as in the creational
world which is phenomenal, difference of degree is an
obstacle or hindrance to comprehension, how can
the human being, which is a created exigency, comprehend the ancient divine reality which is essential?
This is impossible because the reality of divinity is
sanctified beyond the comprehension of the created
being man.

Furthermore, that which man can grasp is finite to
man, and man to it is as infinite. Is it possible then
for the reality of divinity to be finite and the human
creature infinite? On the contrary the reverse is true;
the human is finite while the essence of divinity is
infinite. Whatever comes within the sphere of human
comprehension must be limited and finite. As the
essence of divinity transcends the comprehension of
man, therefore God brings forth certain Manifestations of the divine reality upon whom He bestows
heavenly effulgences in order that they may be inter-
mediaries between humanity and Himself. These holy
Manifestations or prophets of God are as mirrors
which have acquired illumination from the Sun of
Truth, but the Sun does not descend from its high
zenith and does not effect entrance within the mirror.
In truth this mirror has attained complete polish and
purity until the utmost capacity of reflection has been
developed in it, therefore the Sun of Reality with its

fullest effulgence and splendor is revealed therein. These mirrors are earthly whereas the reality of divinity is in its highest apogee. Although its lights are shining and its heat is manifest in them, although these mirrors are telling their story of its effulgence, the Sun nevertheless remains in its own lofty station; it does not descend, it does not effect entrance, because it is holy and sanctified.

The Sun of Divinity and of Reality has revealed itself in various mirrors. Though these mirrors are many, yet the Sun is one. The bestowals of God are one; the reality of the divine religion is one. Consider how the one and same light has reflected itself in the different mirrors or manifestations of it. There are certain souls who are lovers of the Sun; they perceive the effulgence of the Sun from every mirror. They are not fettered or attached to the mirrors; they are attached to the Sun itself and adore it no matter from what point it may shine. But those who adore the mirror and are attached to it, become deprived of witnessing the light of the Sun when it shines forth from another mirror. For instance, the Sun of Reality revealed itself from the Mosaic mirror. The people who were sincere accepted and believed in it. When the same Sun shone from the Messianic mirror, the Jews who were not lovers of the Sun and who were fettered by their adoration of the mirror of Moses did not perceive the lights and effulgences of the Sun of Reality resplendent in Jesus, therefore they were deprived of its bestowals. Yet the Sun of Reality, the Word of God shone from the Messianic mirror through the wonderful channel of Jesus Christ more fully and more wonderfully. Its effulgences were manifestly radiant but even to this day the Jews are holding to the Mosaic mirror. Therefore they are bereft of witnessing the lights of eternity in Jesus.

In brief; the sun is one sun, the light is one light which shines upon all phenomenal being. Every creature has a portion thereof, but the pure mirror can reveal the story of its bounty more fully and completely. Therefore we must adore the light of the Sun no matter through what mirror it may be revealed. We must not entertain prejudice, for prejudice is an obstacle to realization. Inasmuch as the effulgence is one effulgence, the human realities must all become recipients of the same light, recognizing in it the compelling force that unites them in its illumination.

As this is the radiant century, it is my hope that the Sun of Truth may illumine all humanity. May the eyes be opened and the ears become attentive; may souls become resuscitated and consort together in the utmost harmony as recipients of the same light.

Promulgation of Universal Peace.

The World of God

I AM exceedingly happy to meet you. Praise be to God! I see before me souls who have unusual capability and the power of spiritual advancement. In reality, the people of this continent [1] possess great capacity; they are the cause of my happiness and I ever pray that God may confirm and assist them to progress in all the degrees of existence. As they have advanced along material lines, may they develop in idealistic degrees, for material advancement is fruit-

[1] North America.

less without spiritual progress and not productive of everlasting results. For example, no matter how much the physical body of man is trained and developed, there will be no real progression in the human station unless the mind correspondingly advances. No matter how much man may acquire material virtues, he will not be able to realize and express the highest possibilities of life without spiritual graces. God has created all earthly things under a law of progression in material degrees but He has created man and endowed him with powers of advancement toward spiritual and transcendental kingdoms. He has not created material phenomena after His own image and likeness but He has created man after that image and with potential power to attain that likeness. He has distinguished man above all other created things. All created things except man are captives of nature and the sense world but in man there has been created an ideal power by which he may perceive intellectual or spiritual realities. He has brought forth everything necessary for the life of this world but man is a creation intended for the reflection of virtues divine. Consider that the highest type of creation below man is the animal, which is superior to all degrees of life except man. Manifestly the animal has been created for the life of this world. Its highest virtue is to express excellence in the material plane of existence. The animal is perfect when its body is healthy and its physical senses are whole. When it is characterized by the attributes of physical health, when its physical forces are in working order, when food and surrounding conditions minister to its needs, it has attained the ultimate perfection of its kingdom. But man does not depend upon these things for his virtues. No matter how perfect his health and physical powers, if that is all, he has not yet risen above the degree of a perfect animal. Beyond and above this, God has opened the doors of ideal virtues and attainments before the face of man. He has created in his being the mysteries of the divine kingdom. He has bestowed upon him the power of intellect so that through the attribute of reason when fortified by the Holy Spirit he may penetrate and discover ideal realities and become informed of the mysteries of the world of significances. As this power to penetrate the ideal knowledge is superhuman, supernatural, man becomes the collective center of spiritual as well as material forces, so that the divine spirit may manifest itself in his being, the effulgences of the Kingdom shine within the sanctuary of his heart, the signs of the attributes and perfections of God reveal themselves in a newness of life, the glory everlasting and existence eternal be attained, the knowledge of God illumine, and the mysteries of the realm of might be unsealed.

Man is like unto this lamp; but the effulgences of the Kingdom are like the rays of the lamp. Man is like unto the glass; but spiritual splendors are like unto the light within the glass. No matter how translucent the glass may be, as long as there is no light within, it remains dark. Likewise man, no matter how much he advances in material accomplishments, he will remain like the glass without light if he is deprived of the virtues spiritual. Material virtues are like unto a perfect body but this body is in need of the spirit. No matter how handsome and perfect the body may be, if it is deprived of the spirit and its animus, it is dead. But when that same body is affiliated with the spirit and expessing life, perfection and

virtue become realized in it. Deprived of the Holy
Spirit and its bounties, man is spiritually dead.

Children, for instance, no matter how good and
pure, no matter how healthy their bodies, they are
nevertheless considered imperfect because the power
of intellect is not fully manifest in them. When the
intellectual power fully displays its influences and
they attain to the age of maturity, they are considered as perfect. Likewise man, no matter how much
he may advance in worldly affairs and make progress
in material civilization, is imperfect unless he is
quickened by the bounties of the Holy Spirit; for it
is evident that until he receives that divine impetus
he is ignorant and deprived. . . . But if he is baptized with the Holy Spirit, if he is freed from the
bondage of nature, released from animalistic tendencies and advanced in the human realm, he is fitted
to enter into the divine kingdom. The world of the
kingdom is the realm of divine bestowals and the
bounties of God. It is attainment of the highest
virtues of humanity; it is nearness to God; it is
capacity to receive the bounties of the ancient Lord.
When man advances to this station he attains the
second birth. Before his first or physical birth man
was in the world of the matrix. He had no knowledge
of this world, his eyes could not see; his ears could
not hear. When he was born from the world of the
matrix he beheld another world. The sun was shining
with its splendors, the moon radiant in the heavens,
the stars twinkling in the expansive firmament, the
seas surging, trees verdant and green, all kinds of
creatures enjoying life here, infinite bounties pre-
pared for him. In the world of the matrix, none of
these things existed. In that world he had no knowl-

edge of this vast range of existence, nay, rather, he would have denied the reality of this world. But after his birth he began to open his eyes and behold the wonders of this illimitable universe. Similarly, as long as man is in the matrix of the human world, as long as he is the captive of nature he is out of touch and without knowledge of the universe of the Kingdom. If he attains rebirth while in the world of nature he will become informed of the divine world. He will observe that another and a higher world exists. Wonderful bounties descend, eternal life awaits, everlasting glory surrounds him. All the signs of reality and greatness are there. He will see the lights of God. All these experiences will be his when he is born out of the world of nature into the world divine. Therefore for the perfect man there are two kinds of birth. The first, physical birth, is from the matrix of the mother; the second or spiritual birth is from the world of nature. In both he is without knowledge of the new world of existence he is entering. Therefore rebirth means his release from the captivity of nature, freedom from attachment to this mortal and material life. This is the second or spiritual birth of which His Holiness Jesus Christ spoke in the gospels.

The majority of people are captives in the matrix of nature, submerged in the sea of materiality. We must pray that they may be reborn, that they may attain insight and spiritual hearing, that they may receive the gift of another heart, a new transcendent power, and in the eternal world the unending bestowal of divine bounties.

Today the world of humanity is walking in darkness because it is out of touch with the world of God. That is why we do not see the signs of God in the hearts of men. The power of the Holy Spirit has no influence. When a divine spiritual illumination becomes manifest in the world of humanity, when divine instruction and guidance appear, then enlightenment follows, a new spirit is realized within, a new power descends and a new life is given. It is like the birth from the animal kingdom into the kingdom of man. When man acquires these virtues, the oneness of the world of humanity will be revealed, the banner of international peace will be upraised, equality between all mankind will be realized and the Orient and Occident will become one. Then will the justice of God become manifest, all humanity will appear as the members of one family and every member of that family will be consecrated to cooperation and mutual assistance. The lights of the love of God will shine; eternal happiness will be unveiled; everlasting joy and spiritual delight will be attained.

I will pray and you must pray likewise that such heavenly bounty may be realized; that strife and enmity may be banished, warfare and bloodshed taken away; that hearts may attain ideal communication and that all people may drink from the same fountain. May they receive their knowledge from the same divine source. May all hearts become illumined with the rays of the Sun of Reality; all of them enter the university of God, acquire spiritual virtues and seek for themselves heavenly bounties. Then this material, phenomenal world will become the mirror of the world of God and within this pure mirror the divine virtues of the realm of might will be reflected.

Promulgation of Universal Peace.